THE DOG IS NOT A TOY
(HOUSE RULE #4)

THE DOG IS NOT A TOY
(HOUSE RULE #4)

by

Darby Conley

Andrews McMeel
Publishing

Kansas City

To my mom and dad

who laughed when they were supposed to.

7

13

18

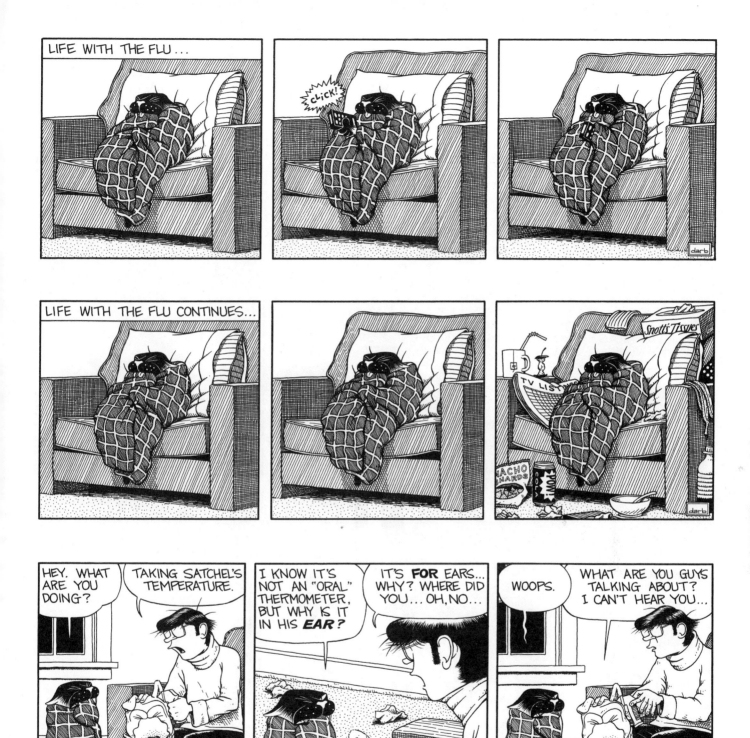

20

24

BUCKY SAYS HE'S GONNA BE IN A TV AD...

NOT IF I CAN HELP IT.

HE'S BEEN SHOWING ME ALL THE FREEBIES HE GOT FROM THE TOOL COMPANY.

WHAT "FREEBIES"?

BUCKY, I DECIDED THAT YOU CAN'T DO THE ADS FOR "SPARKY TOOLS." WE'LL HAVE TO RETURN THESE FREE TOOLS.

AW, MANNN.

EEW! THIS SANDER IS COVERED IN... WHAT IS THIS, MEAT?!

THE HAM WAS FATTY... I TRIMMED IT.

?

YOU EVER WONDER WHAT HE CARRIES AROUND IN THAT BACKPACK?

UMMM... NNNO...

DID MS. PRETTY LIKE OUR TRIP TO THE YARD? WOULD MS. PRETTY LIKE SOME TEA NOW?

35

36

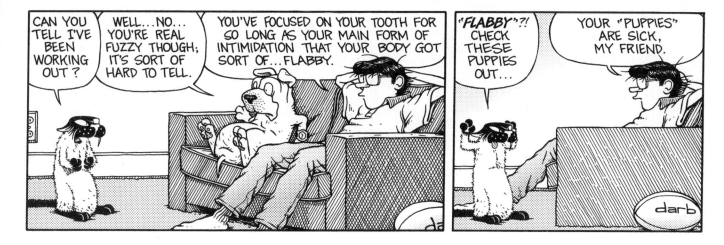

43

44

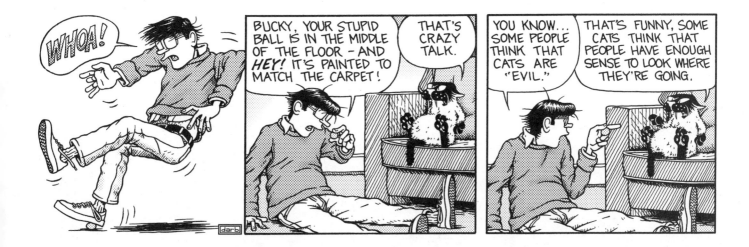

57

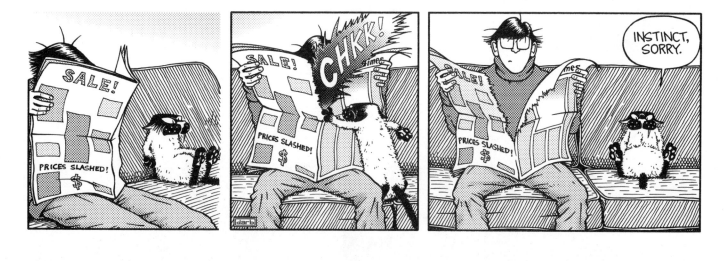

68

70

71

SO WHY DIDN'T YOU LIKE MY BOOK?

IT'S NOT "BAD," YOU JUST NEED TO HAVE SOMETHING TO *TALK ABOUT*, LIKE A PERSONAL TRAGEDY OR TRIUMPH...

"TRAGEDY OR TRIUMPH"? JEEZ, YOU REALLY DON'T LET ME OUT THAT MUCH...

WHAT IF SOMETHING TRAGIC HAPPENED TO **SATCHEL**, COULD I WRITE ABOUT THAT?

NO.

CAN YOU MAIL THIS FOR ME? I'M SENDING MY MANUSCRIPT TO A PUBLISHER.

SURE... WHY IS IT SO LUMPY?

I FIGURED IT WOULDN'T HURT TO BUTTER THE EDITOR UP WITH A GIFT.

I DON'T WANT TO KNOW WHAT IT IS, DO I?

WHY NOT? *OH*, NO, DON'T WORRY, IT'S ALREADY DEAD.

IF YOU SAY THAT ONE MORE TIME, I'LL-- *STOP SAYING THAT!* ARE YOU LISTENING TO ME?! HEY!. BE **QUIET!**

YOU'D BETTER DO SOMETHING ABOUT BUCKY; HE'S YELLING AT SOMEONE ON THE PHONE.

SERIOUSLY? HA HA HA!!

WHY ARE YOU LAUGHING? HE'S REALLY SCREAMING AT SOMEBODY.

NO, NO - HE MADE ME CALL A PUBLISHER ABOUT HIS "BOOK," AND THEN YANKED THE PHONE AWAY FROM ME AND STARTED YELLING AT A RECORDED MESSAGE... HE STARTED AN *HOUR* AGO!

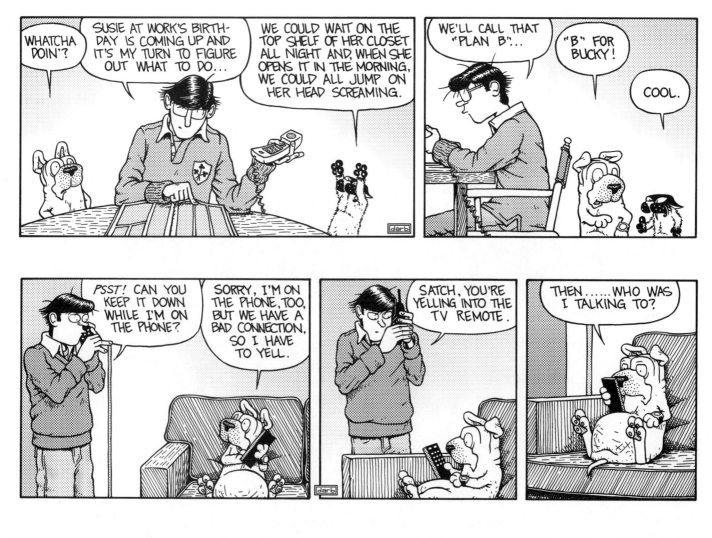

WHATCHA DOIN'?

SUSIE AT WORK'S BIRTHDAY IS COMING UP AND IT'S MY TURN TO FIGURE OUT WHAT TO DO...

WE COULD WAIT ON THE TOP SHELF OF HER CLOSET ALL NIGHT AND, WHEN SHE OPENS IT IN THE MORNING, WE COULD ALL JUMP ON HER HEAD SCREAMING.

WE'LL CALL THAT "PLAN B"...

"B" FOR BUCKY!

COOL.

PSST! CAN YOU KEEP IT DOWN WHILE I'M ON THE PHONE?

SORRY, I'M ON THE PHONE, TOO, BUT WE HAVE A BAD CONNECTION, SO I HAVE TO YELL.

SATCH, YOU'RE YELLING INTO THE TV REMOTE.

THEN......WHO WAS I TALKING TO?

ROB?...HI! LONG TIME NO SEE!

HI, JANICE, YEAH, IT'S BEEN A WHILE.

OH, AND HERE'S LITTLE *BUCKY.* HE'S SO CUTE IN HIS LITTLE CARRIER--NOW BE HONEST, ROB, YOU JUST CARRY HIM AROUND TO MEET WOMEN, DON'T YOU?

YOUR HAIR USED TO BE **ALL** DARK...NOW IT FADES FROM BLACK TO WHITE.....LIKE A GERMAN SHEPHERD. I DON'T LIKE IT.

I DON'T MEET MANY WOMEN THIS WAY.

80

83

SO I'M GOING TO THE RALLY... CAN I HAVE TWENTY BUCKS?

$20?! YOU'RE NOT ONLY A CAT, YOU'RE A *HIPPIE* CAT!

BUT, *ROB!* ACTIVISM COSTS MONEY! I NEED CAB FARE AND A *MEGAPHONE!*

HERE'S 85 CENTS -TAKE THE BUS AND SCREAM YOUR LUNGS OUT.

I GIVE IT HALF AN HOUR BEFORE THE CROWD FREAKS HIM OUT AND HE BITES SOMEBODY.

I DIDN'T EVEN THINK HE *LIKED* OTHER CATS.

HEYYY! THERE'S THE LITTLE ACTIVIST! HOW WAS THE RALLY?

NOT SO GOOD. WE GOT TO CITY HALL OK, BUT WHEN THE ALPHA CAT WENT TO SPEAK, HIS MEGAPHONE WAS SCREWING UP...

SO?

WELL... THE FEEDBACK FREAKED OUT ALL THE OTHER CATS... MOST OF US ENDED UP IN TRASH CANS OR UP TREES... I HID UNDER A CAR FOR TWO HOURS AND THEN I RAN HOME.

YOU DID THE RIGHT THING, BUCKY.

WELL, I'M SORRY TO HEAR THAT YOUR BIG PROTEST MARCH DIDN'T GO WELL. I COULD HAVE TOLD YOU THAT USING A SCREECHY MEGAPHONE ON A BUNCH OF WORKED-UP CATS WAS A RECIPE FOR DISASTER.

IT WASN'T A TOTAL LOSS... I GOT A T-SHIRT...

CHAT GUEVARA. CUTE.

89

91

92

97

118

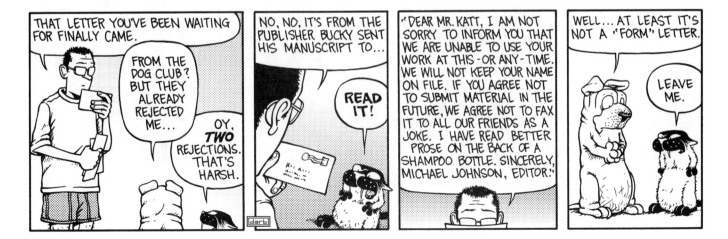